Other Nitty Gritty Cookbooks

Classical Greek Cooking
Low Carbohydrate Cookbook
The Compleat American
  Housewife 1776
Kid's Cookbook
The World in One Meal
The Italian Cookbook
The Cheese Guide and Cookbook
The First Brandy Cookbook
To My Daughter, With Love
Quiches and Souffles
Miller's German Cookbook
The Natural Foods Cookbook
The Chinese Vegetarian Cookbook
Four Seasons Party Cookbook

The Jewish Gourmet Cookbook
Working Couples Cookbook
The Mexican Cookbook
Paris and Then Some Cookbook
Sunday Breakfast Cookbook
Fisherman's Wharf Cookbook
Charcoal Cookbook
Ice Cream Cookbook
Hippo Hamburger Cookbook
Gourmet Blender Cookbook
Wok Cookbook
Christmas Cookbook
Cast Iron Cookbook
Japanese Country Cookbook
The Fondue Cookbook

To my husband Pete, the plant waterer, to my son Jimmy, the seed grower, and to my daughter Jan, the plant watcher.

Love,
Rosemary

To my husband Don, greenhouse-builder and plant enthusiast, to my Dad and Mom, and to Gerry and Debi Podesta for giving invaluable help.

Pat

The Kids Garden Book

Written by Patricia Petrich and Rosemary Dalton
Spot illustrations by Patricia Petrich
Full page art by Young Artists

Library of Congress Cataloging in Publication Data

Petrich, Patricia.
   The kids garden book.

   SUMMARY: Basic information about tools, light,
containers, soil, seed beds, and other aspects of gardening with directions for planting and caring for ferns,
cactus, popcorn, gourds, and many other plants.
   1. Gardening--Juvenile literature. [1. Gardening]
I. Dalton, Rosemary, joint author. II. Title.
SB457.P47   635   74-17230
ISBN 0-911954-32-5

Contents

Hi Gardeners-to-be,

We hope you like this garden book and will have fun growing things and enjoying them too. If you are an older kid we're sure you can garden pretty much on your own, using experienced gardeners as a resource when necessary. If you are younger, you will need the help of parents or older brothers and sisters to do some projects.

Planning what to grow is half the fun. And the plants you grow yourself will be the best ever!

1. Anyone can enjoy the world of gardening — indoors and out. Good ways to get started are looking at plants, visiting places where they grow, and talking to people who grow them. You will learn a lot before you know it — and you'll have fun too!

2. Try not to feel too bad if you have problems or a plant dies. Everyone who gardens has these things happen. Try to find out what went wrong — Next time will be better!

2

Rules for a Good Green Thumb (cont.)

3. Get an okay on all your plant projects before you start. Someone may not like your Venus Fly-trap lurking in the living room. Be sure to read all seed packets and plant directions. Get help when necessary.

4. When working on potting or repotting plants inside, make sure to put down newspapers before you start.

Rules for a Good Green Thumb (cont.)

5. Put garden tools away and clean up when finished for the day. Wiping your feet before going in the house is a good idea too.

6. You will be more popular around the house if you keep saucers under your houseplants. They can drip a lot!

clunk....

Rules for a Good Green Thumb (cont.)

7. Never eat leaves, berries, or other parts of plants (unless you get an okay from an adult who knows it is safe)! Many plants are poisonous — not safe to munch on!

8. Enjoy the world of gardening and watching things grow— you can have fun sharing your plants and cuttings with friends. They might decide to garden too!

Garden Tools

Rake		Used to smooth out soil, clean-up.
Hoe		Used for weeding, loosening the soil.
Trowel		Used for scooping soil, digging holes.
Spade		Used to dig the soil, make holes.
Hat, gloves	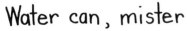	Used to save you sunburn and blisters!
Water can, mister		Used to water indoor plants and to "spray" or "mist" them.

Garden Terms

thin the plants

Cut some plants or pull them out as they come up, to leave room for plants to grow.

crocking

To "crock the pot" put a broken piece of clay pot over the flower pot hole for drainage.

filtered light

The kind of light most houseplants like - near a window with a drape, or a little way away from a window.

spray or mist

Spray plant with water. Plants with smooth leaves love it!

Garden Terms (cont.)

fertilize or
"feed" plants

This adds nutrients to the soil, indoors or out.
Get adult help with this if you want to do it.

stem
cutting

When you cut off a piece of the plant and
root it in water or soil you have a "cutting."
It is a new plant.

Parts of a Plant:

flower or
blossom →

stem

leaves

roots

Garden Terms (cont.)

potting soil   Soil especially for indoor plants. There are more sandy potting soils for cactus plants.

seed bed   Place where a lot of plants are started at once, indoors.

pinch   To cut or squeeze off some of the plant. Pinching the flower off a coleus makes it bushy.

transplant   To put the plant in a bigger pot or move it from indoors to the ground outdoors.

Garden Terms (cont.)

fronds — The leafy branches of ferns.

insectivorous — Plants or animals that eat insects.

hydroponics — The science of growing plants in water.

Green Thumb — What you have when you like your plants, take care of them, and they thrive and grow.

Grow 'em Indoors

All plants need soil, air, light and water. You can buy basic potting mix, or special potting mix for cactus plants in supermarkets and nurseries. If you really want to mix your own soil, here are 2 recipes, one basic and one for cactus.

Basic Potting Mix
Equal parts { 1 part packaged potting mix 1 part sand (not ocean sand) or perlite 1 part peat moss

Grow 'em Indoors (cont.)

Cactus plants need more sandy soil.

> ## Cactus Potting Mix
> 1 part packaged basic potting mix
> 2 parts sand (not ocean sand) *

    Whether you mix your own soil or get a packaged soil mix, you will have soil that will be good for your plants. Do not use dirt taken from outdoors, as it might have insects, weed seeds or plant diseases.

* Salt from ocean sand will kill plants.

Soil Chart

This chart tells approximate amounts of soil you need.

Diameter of inside of pot (on top of pot)		Approximate amount of soil needed.	
Standard	Metric	Standard	Metric
2 inches	(5 centimeters)	$\frac{1}{3}$ cup	(92 cubic centimeters)
3 inches	(8 centimeters)	1 cup	(275 cubic centimeters)
4 inches	(10 centimeters)	$2\frac{1}{2}$ cups	(688 cubic centimeters)
5 inches	(13 centimeters)	$4\frac{1}{2}$ cups	(1.24 liters)
6 inches	(15 centimeters)	$2\frac{1}{2}$ quarts	(2.75 liters)
7 inches	(18 centimeters)	3 quarts	(3.30 liters)
8 inches	(20 centimeters)	1 gallon	(4.41 liters)

Grow 'em Indoors (cont.)

These are good rules to follow if you mix your own soil:

1. Find a good work area (where no one minds if you work on something messy).

2. Put down newspaper or plastic.

3. Put amounts of things you need in a mixing bowl. Mix until smooth — no lumps!

4. Wet the soil mix until it is damp (not soggy) all the way through. The chart on p. 15 will show you about how much soil you need.

5. Be sure to clean up your mess!

How to Plant a Seed Bed

If you are planting a lot of seeds indoors you need a seed bed. This is a place where many plants are started. Then they are "thinned out", and the best and the strongest grow into seedlings. Seedlings are then transplanted into their own pots or into soil outdoors.

This is a seed bed. ↑

You need:
Packet of seeds
Container + soil
Adult help if
necessary

This is not a seed bed. ↖

18

How to Make a Seed Bed (cont.)

To make a seed bed, follow these steps:

1. Pick a container. Punch holes in the bottom. Here are some ideas for containers.

Cut side off.

Milk Carton

cut↓

Bleach

Take top off.

COFFEE

Take bottom off.
Put plastic lid back on.

Plastic Ice Cream Tub

Ice Cream

2. Put a layer of pebbles in the bottom of the container for drainage.

How to Make a Seed Bed (cont.)

3. Mix potting soil with water in a mixing bowl until the soil is damp. Fill your container with potting mix to $\frac{1}{2}$ inch from the top.

4. Read the seed packet to see how far apart to plant seeds, and how deep. Cover seeds gently with dirt. Spray very lightly with water.

5. Cover your seed bed with clear plastic wrap. Put the container in a place with filtered light. (No direct sunlight). Keep something (aluminum foil tray, old plate) under punched holes so the container won't leak.

"Spraying" or "misting"

How to Make a Seed Bed (cont.)

6. Keep your seed bed well watered, but don't drown the seeds. *blub*

7. Take off the plastic wrap when little leaves appear.

8. When seeds start to grow take a . scissors and cut off enough plants so that leaves do not touch each other. This is called "thinning". When your seedlings have 2 or 3 sets of leaves you are ready to "transplant".

snip *snip*

Thinning

Moving Day for Plants
(Transplanting)

You will be transplanting when any of these things happen.

Large seed-lings need a new home.

Plant cutting has roots and needs to be planted in soil.

Plant roots grow out of the bottom of the pot or poke out of the top of the pot.

roots →

How to Transplant

1. Plants need good drainage in any new home. If you are putting your plant into a larger clay pot put a piece of a broken clay pot over the hole. (This is called crocking. It lets the water run out). Then put a little bit of soil in the pot.

2. If there is no hole, put a layer of pebbles and a little bit of gardening charcoal on the bottom of the container. Add a bit of soil.

3. If you are planting seedlings, dig into the soil with

How to Transplant (cont.)

a spoon and gently lift each one out.
Keep as much soil on the roots as you
can. They are fragile.

    4. Set the plant into the pot on the
soil. Set in cuttings this way too.

    5. Fill the pot with soil up to $\frac{1}{2}$ inch from
the top. Don't cover the leaves. Push the soil
down gently over the roots of plant.

    6. Water your plant with lukewarm water.
Let the water drain out the bottom of the pot.

    7. If you are moving a plant to a

Moving
day blues

bigger pot you can loosen the soil with a long spatula. Run it along the inside edge of the pot.

It can be hard to get a plant out of its pot.

8. Spank or slap the pot bottom. Then turn it upside down. Keep one hand under the plant leaves to catch your plant. Then pot the plant following the transplanting instructions. Be sure to do this on a table top covered with newspapers, or outside on the ground.

swat

spatula

26

Light

Most houseplants need "filtered light". That means putting your plant near a window with a shade or drape in front of it, or putting it a little way away from the window.

Only cactus plants and a few other plants like direct sunlight. (Right next to a window with the sun shining in).

Plants grow toward the light. Turn the pot often or you will have a leaning plant.

um...
feels good....

Feeding Your Plants

Some people feed their plants once a month or so, (to enrich the soil) and some do not. If you want to do this get adult help, as there are many kinds of plant foods, and many ways of doing this.

Tender Loving Care

Some people talk to their plants or play music for them. Try this if you want to give your plant extra TLC.

Watering Your Plants

Watch out for my leaves!

A fuzzy plant...

Some plants are very thirsty and need lots of water. Some don't need much water at all. Before watering your plant, feel the soil. If it is too damp, don't water. Too much water can kill your plant. (Not enough water can kill it too, but many people over water).

One way to water your plant is to carry it to the sink. It's a good place to let the water drain out. Make sure the water is lukewarm. Use a container with a spout. (Plants with fuzzy leaves don't like water on their leaves).

Water your plant from the top. Add enough water so that it drains out the bottom of the pot. Make sure all the water drains out before putting the plant back on its saucer. The plant roots need air. They should not sit in water.

Plants hate wet feet!

Some plants (but never fuzzy leaved ones) need their leaves "sprayed" or "misted" with water. A plastic spray bottle works fine. Plants like this because air indoors gets dry.

If you have a hanging plant, one way to water is with ice cubes. Put a "necklace" of ice cubes around

Watering Your Plants (cont.)

the rim of the pot. The ice will melt slowly and water will not leak out of the pot.

ice cubes

If your plant is in a clay pot, here is a funny way to see if it needs water. Knock on the pot. If the soil is wet, the noise will be "thonk." If the soil is dry, the pot will ring.

Water me.

Not yet, thanks.

Containers

Containers for Your Plants

You can use just about any waterproof container. Use your imagination!

Containers (cont.)

The best containers for your plants have a hole or holes in the bottom for drainage.

When you use a container with a hole, put a piece of broken clay pot over the hole so the water can drain out.

When you use a container without a hole, put a layer of pebbles in the bottom, for drainage.

Containers

Some old toys (wagons, plastic trucks, beach pails, etc.) are great to put plants in! (Get permission first). Or you can pot the plants in clay or plastic flower pots then set them in another container. Some ideas are: an old baby shoe, a shoeskate that doesn't fit, etc.

Look around the house. You will get some ideas of your own.

Containers (cont.)

Plants look good in some of these things too!

old drawers

funnels

wire baskets

old toys

fishbowls

36

Containers (cont.)

coffee can or
ice cream tub +
wrapping paper

milk carton

orange juice
cans

muffin tin

eggshells

seashells

birdcage →

Braided Plant Hanger
Use macramé knots or beads too, if you like.)

Cut the twine into 6 pieces. Make each piece 9 feet long. Hold the pieces so they are all even. ≡ Fold them in half. ⊂ Tie a knot at the top. Leave a loop. Put the loop under a chairleg or someplace it will be held tight.

You need:
1 roll of jute, twine or string (54 feet or longer—check the label).
scissors
ruler or yardstick

Separate the twine into 4 groups of 3 strings. Braid each group. Tie a knot under all 4 braids and put your pot in the hanger. Or make the wooden pot hanger on the next page.

Wooden Plant Hanger
Use this with the braided hanger on p. 38.

Buy 1 piece of $\frac{3}{4}$ inch by $\frac{3}{4}$ inch Redwood 3 feet long. Have it cut into 4 pieces 9 inches long. Nail the 4 pieces together like this, 2 pieces on top, 2 on the bottom. Leave $5\frac{1}{2}$ inches between each piece. Nail in a place where you won't hurt anything. Get adult help if needed.

Tie the loose ends of your braided plant hanger to the 4 <u>bottom</u> corners of the wood. Have someone hang it for you. You can use it indoors or out. Your hanger fits a 6 inch size pot.

39

Plants from Throw-Aways

There are many plants you can grow from things you throw away — pineapple tops, avocado seeds, and many more. You can have a big garden just from saving seeds and tops from things you eat!

Carrot Top Plant
A lacy green plant

Cut about 2 inches off the sprouted top of a carrot.*
Cut the leaves off too. Put the carrot top, cut side down, in a shallow dish with water in it. Change the water often. Keep it $\frac{1}{2}$ inch deep. When roots appear, plant the carrot, cut side down, in a pot filled with moist sand. Keep your new plant well watered, and put it in a sunny window. It will look a lot like a fern.

* Have someone help you cut the carrot, if necessary.

42

Beet Top Plant

This plant has dark green leaves with red veins.

Grow this plant just like the carrot top. Cut off the beet top and put it in a dish of water to root. When roots appear, plant the beet top in a pot or container filled with moist sand.

You can grow plants from turnips and parsnips this way too.

Keep your plants in a sunny spot, and water them well.

Citrus Fruit Plants
Easy to Grow!

You need:

Seeds from lemons, oranges, or grapefruits

4 inch pot

Basic potting soil

Soak the seeds in water overnight. Then plant them about 1 inch deep in potting soil and water them. Plant 2 or 3 seeds in each pot. Label the pots so you know which is which.

Put the pots in a sunny window. Water every few days. Turn pots so plants don't bend toward the light.

Avocado Plant
Eat the avocado but save the pit!

You need:
Avocado pit
Pot and potting
  soil
  or
Glass of water
and 3 toothpicks
to hold up the
pit.

You can start the avocado pit in a glass of water, but it is easiest to start right in a pot full of potting soil.

Let the avocado pit dry out for a day or so. Peel off the brown covering. Put the pit in a pot of potting soil with the pointed end up. Leave some of the pit peeking out until your plant starts to grow. Then cover it with soil. Keep it in a sunny spot or outdoors. It needs lots of water.

Hanging Basket Carrot
Great for a window garden!

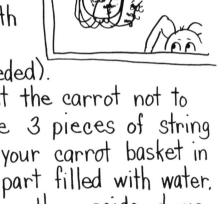

Cut about 2 inches off a big, thick carrot top. Break off the green leaves. Make 3 holes about ½ inch from the cut edge with a thin nail. Hollow out the center of the carrot with a sharp knife. (Get help if needed).

Be careful when hollowing out the carrot not to get too near the outside. Tie 3 pieces of string in the nail holes, and hang your carrot basket in the window. Keep the hollow part filled with water.

Watch for leaves to sprout from the upside-down carrot top. They will turn upward as they grow.

½ - 2 inch hollow

47

Pineapple Plant

Cut the top of a pineapple off with about 1 inch of fruit attached. Cut out the fruit from under the leaves. (This is hard to cut. Get help if needed).

Let the pineapple top dry out for a day or two. Then put it in a shallow dish filled with moist sand. Keep the sand damp. The pineapple will root in 5-8 weeks. Then repot it in a large pot in basic potting soil. Keep the pot in a sunny window. Water it often. Water right on the leaves. Your plant is growing well when it has stiff prickly leaves.

You need:
Pineapple
Knife + adult help
Dish of moist sand

Pineapple Plant (cont.)

If you want your pineapple plant to flower or grow fruit, put several slices of apple on the soil around the plant. Put the pineapple plant in a large plastic bag and keep it tightly closed for 4-5 days. The apple gives off ethylene gas fumes (harmless to people). These fumes cause the pineapple to bloom. A new little pineapple will grow about 6 inches above the old plant. You can pick it and eat it in 3 or 4 months!

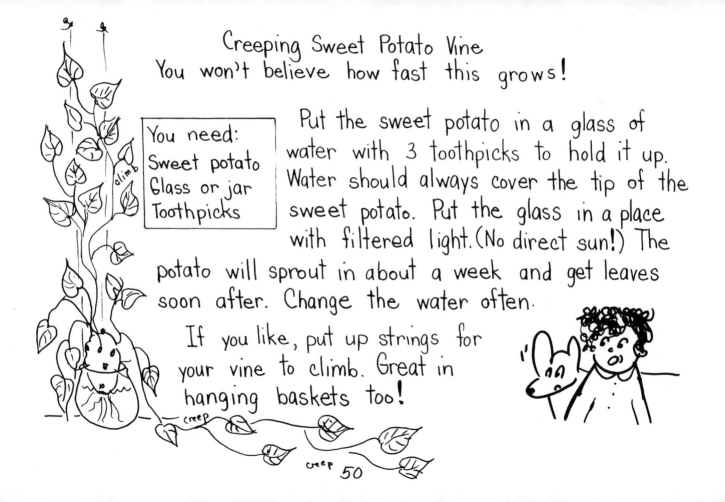

Creeping Sweet Potato Vine
You won't believe how fast this grows!

You need:
Sweet potato
Glass or jar
Toothpicks

Put the sweet potato in a glass of water with 3 toothpicks to hold it up. Water should always cover the tip of the sweet potato. Put the glass in a place with filtered light. (No direct sun!) The potato will sprout in about a week and get leaves soon after. Change the water often.

If you like, put up strings for your vine to climb. Great in hanging baskets too!

creep 50

Garlic Plant
A good present — handy in the kitchen!

This plant is not really started from something you would throw away, but you can start it easily without buying seeds. All you need is 3-4 <u>unpeeled</u> cloves of garlic and a potful of potting soil. Put the cloves in soil at the top of the pot with the points of the cloves up. Barely cover the cloves with soil. Water well.

The garlic plant is very handy to have in the kitchen. Whenever your family needs garlic to season food just snip off little bits of the plant (like chives), and add them to food. Good garlic flavor. The shoots will keep growing so snip often!

51

Indoor Plants

Indoor Plants

You can start most of the plants in this chapter from "stem cuttings" or buy them for a very small amount of money in supermarkets and nurseries. There are a few plants that cost a bit more – try these as you gain experience in gardening.

To make a stem cutting, start with a healthy plant. Cut a piece off (stem + 2 leaves) just below where the leaf joins the stem.

snip

Taking a stem cutting

Indoor Plants (cont.)

Put the cuttings in water* to root. When roots have sprouted, plant in potting soil. (Remember to put drainage material at the bottom). Some plants that are easy to grow from cuttings are Coleus, Aluminum Plant, Chinese Evergreen, Creeping Charlie, Wandering Jew, and Umbrella Tree.

Creating a new life....

*A few kinds can root right in potting soil. This chapter tells which ones.

Wandering Jew
Looks great in a hanging pot!

This plant has unusual markings and color combinations. Some Wandering Jews are green and purple. Others are combinations of green, white and cream colors. This plant does not like water on its leaves. Keep it in filtered light or semi-shade.

Wandering Jews grow very fast. You can start new plants by taking cuttings (see p. 53). Start these cuttings in water or right in damp potting soil.

Chinese Evergreen

The Chinese Evergreen can grow in poor light indoors, where other plants could not live. It can be kept in filtered light too.

It is a good plant to put in a terrarium or

dish garden because it looks good with other plants. You can put it in a pot with no hole because it is hardy.

Let this plant almost dry out before you water it.

Birds Nest Fern

Ferns love water. Spray or mist them with lukewarm water every day. Keep ferns moist, but never soggy. The leaves of the Birds Nest Fern look like feathers.

new plant

Mother Fern

This is called the Mother Fern because tiny baby plants grow right on its leaves. You can pick the plants off carefully and put them in pots. You will have new little plants.

Boston Fern

Keep the Boston Fern moist, never soggy. Spray the fern with lukewarm water every day.

This fern will need a haircut often. Cut off any brown or yellow fronds (leaves) with a scissors. It won't hurt the plant. Snip carefully. Don't pull.

Keep the Boston Fern in filtered sun, in a place where the fronds can hang down.

Kangaroo Vine

This is a good climbing plant with shiny green leaves. It likes medium sunlight. If you put up strings it will climb them.

Grape Ivy

This plant looks a lot like the Kangaroo Vine but it has smaller, darker green leaves. Pinch back* both plants if you want them to be bushier.

* Pinch back means to cut or squeeze off some of the plant.

60

Asparagus Fern
(Springeri)

The Asparagus Fern needs a hang-ing basket, or a place where its branches can hang down and not touch things.

You can spray or mist this plant with lukewarm water. Keep it moist. Put it in a place with a little shade— not too much sun!

62

Aluminum Plant

The Aluminum Plant is easy to recognize because its leaves are green and aluminum colored. It is a good plant for a terrarium. It grows to be about 9 inches high. Keep it moist.

Artillery Plant

The Artillery Plant is good in terrariums too. It grows close to the soil and has tiny leaves. Keep it moist. It gets its name because it releases its seeds "like a shot," in little clouds of pollen.

Creeping Charlie
Also called Swedish Ivy

This plant grows very fast. It needs a lot of water, and has bright green leaves. Keep it in filtered light. Start new plants from cuttings. Root them in water or potting soil. Easy to start.

Snake Plant

The Snake Plant needs very little water. It stores water in its leaves. Do not overwater!

The Snake Plant can be kept in dim light indoors. It is hardy and can grow in a terrarium or a pot with no hole. Its leaves are tall and stiff.

But it doesn't really look like a snake....

65

Prayer Plant
Also called Maranta or Rabbit Tracks

This plant has big green leaves with brown spots. At night the plant's leaves fold up tight. This is where it gets the name "Prayer Plant".

Keep your Prayer Plant in filtered light. Keep it moist. Mist it with warm water often. This keeps the tips from turning brown. This is a good plant for a terrarium or dish garden.

Umbrella Tree
Also called Octopus Plant or Schefflera

A Super Plant!

This plant has long, dark green leaves that grow like an umbrella at the top of the stem. You can buy a little one and end up with a large plant. It grows fast.

Let the plant dry out before you water it, but spray or mist it every day. This helps keep the plant clean and free from pests.

Surprise Plants

    The world is full of plants that do strange things. Insect eating plants are some of the strangest of all. There are several kinds of insectivorous (insect eating) plants. Two of the most interesting are the Venus Fly-Trap and the Cobra Lily.

    There are many other plants that grow in an interesting way, or do things that surprise us. We have only included a few — see how many you can discover....

I eat it, yum....

Sensitive Plant
Also called Mimosa

This is a very strange plant. If you touch it, the leaves fold up! The leaves fold together and the stems fold down. You can touch the plant many times without hurting it. It will unfold right away!

The Sensitive Plant is very easy to grow from seeds. You can plant them indoors, or outside in warm weather.

This plant has fern-like leaves and small lavender flowers. It likes a sunny spot. Keep it moist.

poke!

Venus Fly-trap
A bug catcher!

The Venus Fly-trap is an insect-eating plant. It has thick, spiky leaves with bristles on the sides. When a fly (or other insect) touches one of these bristles the halves of the leaf begin to fold together. The fly cannot escape.

This plant grows from a bulb. You can order it from garden catalogs (see list on p. 176.) or buy plants at some dime stores or nurseries.

The Venus Fly-trap likes a lot of sun and water. If there is a shortage of flies it can be fed tiny pieces of raw ground meat.

Piggyback

The Piggyback plant has hairy light green leaves. It is fun to have because you can watch the new little plantlets grow right out of the plant's leaves (where the leaf joins the stem).

To start a new plant, cut off a leaf and put it in moist sand (not ocean sand). Roots will sprout. Plant your new Piggyback in potting soil in a small pot. Keep well-watered, but don't get water on the leaves. They will get brown spots. Keep plant in filtered light.

72

Coleus

Plant the coleus seeds in basic potting mix – remember the drainage material. This plant needs plenty of water. Keep it in a sunny place.

The Coleus leaves will be many colors. To start new plants take cuttings (see p. 53) and root them in water.

Coleus plants have a few flowers. Cut them off to keep the plant bushy and full.

Cobra Lily

The Cobra Lily has glands that contain honey. Insects smell it and crawl inside. The plant has barbs so that insects cannot crawl back out. They decay and become food for the plant.

You can get Cobra Lilies from some nurseries or order them by mail (see p. 177). Gotcha!

Keep your cobra plant in filtered sunlight and keep it well watered. It will catch its own food....

Spider Plant
Also called an Airplane Plant

This plant is called a Spider Plant because of the little plants that grow from the "Mother plant." They look like spiders at the end of a web.

The plantlets grow on "runners". They grow and get heavy. To pot these new little Spider Plants, wait until they have roots about $\frac{1}{2}$ inch long. Cut them from the Mother plant. Plant in potting soil. Water well.

Cactus

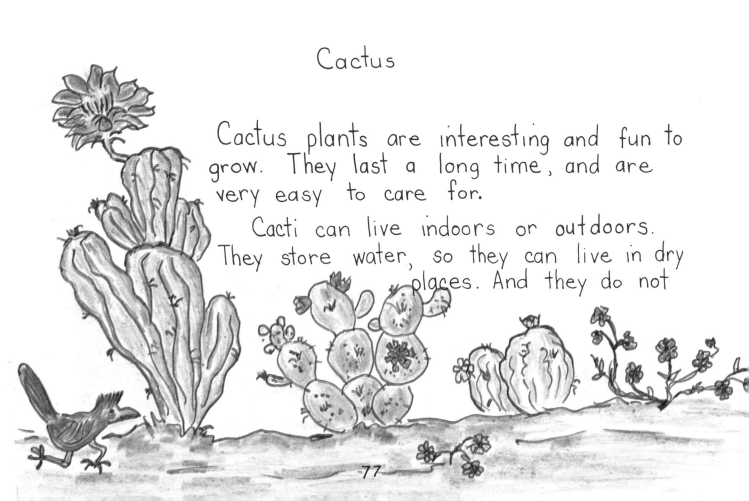

Cactus

Cactus plants are interesting and fun to
grow. They last a long time, and are
very easy to care for.

Cacti can live indoors or outdoors.
They store water, so they can live in dry
places. And they do not

Cactus (cont.)

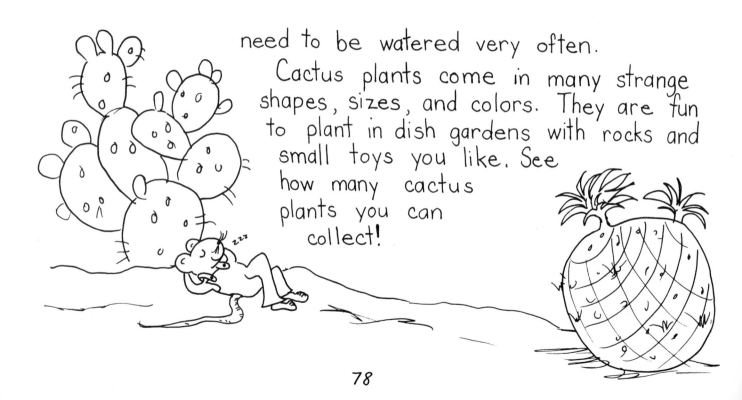

need to be watered very often.

Cactus plants come in many strange shapes, sizes, and colors. They are fun to plant in dish gardens with rocks and small toys you like. See how many cactus plants you can collect!

Cactus Planting

Yow

Cactus plants can be very prickly!
Here are some hints on how to handle
your cactus when planting:

Use a folded newspaper to grab
your cactus plant. This will keep
cactus spines in the cactus and out
of you! Gloves are good too!

Have a spoon handy to use for
moving the soil around the
plant.

Cactus Dish Garden

Make your own Western movie setting or desert scene!

You need:
Cactus plants
Shallow container – size you like
Cactus potting soil
Charcoal bits
Small rocks, decorations or toys to add interest

You can buy little plants for your cactus garden or grow plants from seeds or cuttings. (See p. 158 about cuttings). Pick plants that look good together. A good plan for a dish garden is to use a tall cactus or a short fat one in the center, and put 1 or 2 other plants around it. Then add toys or decorations to finish the scene.

Move along...

Cactus Dish Garden (cont.)

Pick a container that will look good with your plants. Put a small bed of pebbles on the bottom of the container for drainage. Next add a thin layer of charcoal bits. This will keep the soil smelling sweet. Add cactus potting soil. Buy it or mix your own. (Recipe on p. 14).

Set the plants in the container the way you want them. Press the soil down gently. Do not water the plants

soil

charcoal

pebbles

right away. Wait a few days. Then water each plant with a teaspoon until the soil is moist.

Before you water your cactus garden again, test the soil with your finger. If it feels moist, don't water. You don't want the soil to be too wet! This is the best way to tell if your plants need a teaspoon or so of water.

The Before-You-Water Test

Keep your dish garden in a bright spot where there is sun every day. It's fun to watch your small world grow.

Old Man Cactus
Also called Old Lady Cactus or Wooly Cactus

The Old Man Cactus grows very slowly. It is covered with long, gray or white hairs. It has yellow spines. Old plants have rose colored flowers in the Spring.

This is a good container plant. When the plant grows bigger you can put it in your outdoor garden. This cactus can grow to 40 feet tall in the desert!

If you plant this cactus outside, protect it from frost.

Donkey Tail
Also called Burro Tail

One of the fun things to do with cactus is to have a hanging plant. You can start one with 4 inch Donkey Tail cuttings, or several small plants. (See p. 158 about cuttings). When you use several plants your basket will have a nice, full look, especially after the plants grow.

Keep your Donkey Tail in full sun. Let it dry out before watering. (You know it is too dry if the leaves shrivel). You may keep the Donkey Tail outside in warm weather.

Christmas Cactus

Also called Crab's Claw

This plant does very well when started from a cutting. To make a cactus cutting see p. 158.

Keep your Christmas Cactus in the sunlight most of the time. But in the Fall, there is something special to do if you want it to bloom. Keep it in a dark place (no light!) at least 12 hours a night. Do this from September to November because the roots of this plant like to sleep for about 6 weeks. Bring the cactus into the light when it has started to bloom. You should have a bloomin' cactus by Christmas time!

Cactus

Here are some other kinds of cacti you might enjoy growing.

fruit

Peanut Cactus
This cactus has scarlet flowers in Spring.

Prickly Pear Cactus —
This cactus has bright, red fruit.

Barrel Cactus
Cut off the top and it's full of water! Good to know if you're thirsty in the desert.

Teddy Bear Cholla ↓
Looks furry, but is really very prickly!

Cactus (cont.)

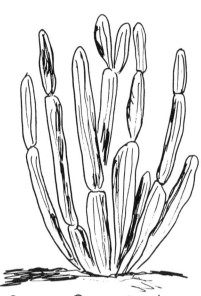

Hedgehog Cactus
has long spines,
big flowers.

Saguaro Cacti
can grow to 50
feet tall, but only
grow a few inches
a year. Many are
100-200 years old.

Organ Pipe Cacti
can grow to 20 feet
tall. Gets night-blooming
flowers high on the stems.

Herbs
Fun to smell....

Herbs are some of the easiest plants to grow! Most herbs grow from seeds. They can be planted in all kinds of small containers (egg shells, clay pots, peat pots, muffin tins, orange juice cans, whatever you like). Be sure to allow for drainage. Seeds are easy to find in grocery stores, nurseries, or wherever seeds are sold.

Herb's Herbs

rosemary   parsley   sage   thyme   basil

Herbs (cont.)

When you grow these herbs and dry them you have good seasonings to add to foods.

To plant herbs use basic potting soil and containers you like. Cover seeds very lightly with soil. Water well. (A good way to water tiny seeds after planting is with a sprayer or mister).

A special way to plant herbs is in a strawberry pot (with pockets) or in a muffin tin. Remember to allow for drainage material.

uh-oh...

sage dressing

Herbs (cont.)

To dry herbs, cut off branches you want to use. Wash in cool water. Dry in a warm, dark room (about 70 degrees) for 2-3 days. Then strip the leaves from the stem. Put each kind of leaf in its own jar. Label each kind so you know what it is. Keep jars covered tightly to preserve the herb. Have fun using your herbs in food. Remember - use just a little bit!

Look in a cookbook to see what foods your herbs are good in.

Just a little bit!

Adventures in Gardening

Adventures in Gardening

If you want to do something special, see this chapter!

Eggshell gardening

Fishland

Your own tiny holiday tree

Easter Basket Garden

Terrariums

A terrarium is a small world of plants — a garden in glass. You can keep it in your room or wherever you like indoors.

Most nurseries have a special section with small plants for terrariums. Some good plants for terrariums are Aluminum Plant, Baby Tears, Snake Plant,

You need:
Glass container ⌂
Gravel or pebbles ∙∙∙
Charcoal   ∙∙∙
Potting soil ▨
Chopsticks or ∥
bent coathanger ⌐
with loop to hold plants
funnel △ or
paper cone (keeps dirt off sides of glass)
terrarium plants

Terrariums (cont.)

Asparagus Fern, etc. To make a terrarium follow these steps.

1. Make paper cone. Add pebbles.

2. 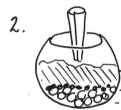 Add charcoal, then soil. (At least 2 inches of soil).

— soil
— charcoal
— pebbles

3. Move soil into high and low levels. Make 2 inch hole.

4. Unpot biggest plant first. Shake off dirt gently.

shake shake

Terrariums (cont.)

5. Lower biggest plant.

6. Tamp down dirt around plant. Add rest of plants the same way.

7. Add twigs, rocks, shells — something to add interest to your little plant world.

8. Water the base of each plant with a straw half filled with water.

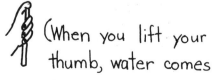

(When you lift your thumb, water comes out.)

Easter Basket Grass
Do this a few weeks before Easter!

Line your Easter basket with aluminum foil. Put in a layer of pebbles for drainage. Add potting soil* to 1 inch from the top. Plant grass seeds (or flowers or herb seeds if you like). When your plants grow tall hide your Easter eggs among them. Happy Egg Hunt!

*If you don't want soil in your basket, put a layer of cotton on the foil. Sprinkle seeds on. Keep cotton moist and seeds will sprout!

97

Growing Plants in Water (Hydroponics)
Root - watching can be fun!

You need:
Container - clear
or colored glass
is good.
Water
Charcoal
Potted plant or
cutting
Plant food will
make your plant
grow faster. Get
adult help to
use it.

If you want to try something different, grow a plant just in water. Some good plants to do this with are Coleus, Piggyback, Chinese Evergreen, Creeping Charlie and Wandering Jew.

If your plant is a cutting it is ready to put in water. If the plant is potted, unpot it and soak the roots in lukewarm water. Rinse them clean. Put the plant in a container with charcoal bits on the bottom. Add water. Cover roots and part of the stem. Change water once a month.

98

Wildflower Gardening

← Dutchman's Breeches

← Shooting Stars

Buttercup

Wildflowers used to grow all over woods and fields. There are not many anymore. Some states have laws so that wildflowers cannot be picked. This is so there will always be some. If you want to preserve and enjoy wildflowers, get seeds from nurseries or from the address on p. 178.

address on p. 178.

Jack-in-the Pulpet

Columbine

Norfolk Island Pine
Also called Star Pine

This little tree is meant especially for growing in the house. It is great to decorate for all holidays – ornaments or cookies for Christmas, hearts for Valentines Day, decorated blown-out eggs for Easter, tiny witches and pumpkins for Halloween. (You can think of other things too!)

Give the tree medium light. Let it dry out between waterings. Repot every 2-3 years.

Fishland
A super plant idea!

You need:
1 <u>Big</u> glass container
Fish
Flower pot
1 small glass terrarium that fits inside the big bowl
Terrarium plants
Charcoal, pebbles, potting soil
Fish food
Water
Water plants from a Fish Store (If you like).

Plant a terrarium following the directions on p. 94. Put the flower pot in the big container upside down. Add rocks and a few water plants to this big bowl. Put the terrarium on the flower pot.

Add water (slowly and carefully) to the big bowl. Keep the water-level 2 inches below the top of the terrarium. This will keep the

102

water from getting into the terrarium.

Put your fish in last. They won't believe their eyes!

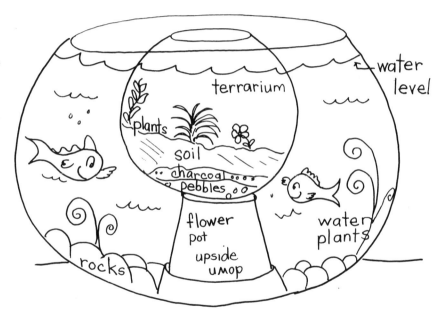

terrarium

water level

plants

soil

charcoal

pebbles

flower pot upside uʍop

water plants

rocks

Turtle Garden
A Park for your turtle!

An aquarium tank is a good container for your turtle terrarium.

Turtles need a little water for swimming, and a big rock to sun on. The plants need to be higher than the water for your turtle. To make the plants higher put down a small bed of rocks in the places you want plants. Then put

You need:
Aquarium tank
Rocks
Plants in containers with <u>no</u> hole

Tiny ceramic or plastic animals for your park (If you like)
Turtle

your plants (leaving them in the containers) on the rocks. Add a turtle, and let him have fun!

<u>Special Added Attractions</u>:

Create other plant or animal worlds with plants and small animals, such as a snake, lizard, or horned toad. (Be sure to get permission before you come home with a pet!)

Eggshell Gardening

Save eggshells. Wash and dry them.
Make a pinhole in the bottom of each one
for drainage. If you want colored shells, dip in
egg dye and let dry.

Put the dry shells in the egg carton. Put
a few pebbles in the bottom of each eggshell. Add potting soil. Plant 2 or 3 seeds
in each shell. Cover lightly with soil. Water
with a teaspoon. This is a great way to
start plants indoors. (Transplant later). Don't
let egg cartons get full of water. Hang your
egg garden with yarn if you like.

You need:
Eggshell halves
Pebbles
Potting soil
Egg carton
Egg dye
Seeds - for
herbs or
flowers.

Flowers from Bulbs Indoors
If you don't have a bowl use a tuna can!

You need:

Shallow bowl
(4-5 inches
high - no hole)
Pebbles or
 stones
Charcoal bits
Water
3-5 large
Narcissus
 bulbs

Line the bowl with about 1-2 inches of pebbles. Put the bulbs on top of them flat end (root end) down. The bulbs should be close together but not touching. Add charcoal bits to keep the water sweet. Put in more pebbles until only about $\frac{1}{2}$ inch of the bulbs stick up. Pour water in until it touches the bottom of the bulbs. Keep the water at this level.

Put the pot in a cool, dark place for 2-3 weeks for bulbs to root. Put the pot in a sunny window when the top of the bulb sprouts. You should have flowers in about 2 weeks!

Grow 'em Outdoors

Grow 'em Outdoors

There are many ways to garden outdoors. You can grow plants in containers, using potting soil, or plant them right in prepared soil in your yard. Plan your garden in rows, circles, or any shape you like. Plan it in an area with 6-8 hours of sun daily. Leave enough space between plants that you can get in there to weed and water.

You can plant bulbs, seeds, seedlings or seed tapes. (Seed tapes are

fun to try. They are easy to handle because the seeds are already set in, and spaced, in tapes). There are seed tapes for flowers, vegetables and herbs.

Another easy way to garden is to use indoor starter kits. There are starter kits for many flowers and vegetables. All you need to do is punch holes in the containers and water the plants. (Transplant when seedlings are sturdy).

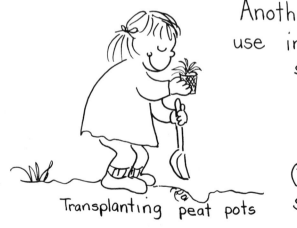

Transplanting peat pots

Garden Plans

Peat pots can also be purchased for starting plants indoors. When the seedlings are ready to be transplanted outdoors, just plant the whole peat pot in the ground. The plant roots will keep on growing right through the peat pot.

Before you prepare your soil for gardening outdoors, first plan the size and shape of your garden. Plan to plant things you and your family enjoy or like to eat. Plan things that will grow in your climate and in the amount of space you have.

111

Grow 'em Outdoors (cont.)

Start in early Spring. Pull out all weeds by the roots. Turn the soil with a shovel or spade. Break up any big lumps, and rake the ground until smooth. (This is a <u>big</u> job. Get help if you can!)

Vegetables need to be grown in well-drained soil and in full sun. They need lots of nutrients in the soil. One way to enrich your soil is to use fertilizer. Have your Dad or Mom or another adult fertilize the ground for you.

Grow 'em Outdoors (cont.)

Before planting, wet the soil so it is moist at least 1 foot down. Pick up a handful and form it into a ball. The soil should be loose and crumbly. If so, you are ready to plant. Remember to keep the weeds out of your garden!

Mini - Gardening
Midget Fruits and Vegetables are fun to grow!

There are many kinds of midget fruits and vegetables that you can grow in containers or small gardens. You can even grow some of them indoors on a windowsill, or in a hanging basket. Midget beets, carrots, radishes, lettuce and tomatoes will grow very well in a sunny window. Tubs and wood planters are good for planting small squash and cucumbers.

Tiny Tim Tomatoes

You can get midget seeds or pre-started plants from nurseries or send for a catalog from the

Mini - Gardening (cont.)

address on p. 177. Some other kinds of midget vegetables and fruits are pumpkins, watermelons peas, cantaloupes, sweet corn, popcorn, eggplants, cabbage and peppers. You can have your own farm with just some midget seeds and a few pots!

Whether you grow tiny plants or regular-sized ones give them sun, water, and soil with good drainage. You'll soon be eating food that tastes much better than fruits and vegetables from the store!

GROWING FLOWERS

Growing Flowers

Flowers are exciting to grow because they come in so many different colors. You can plant them from seeds, seed tapes or bulbs. A bulb looks like an onion* but is really a storehouse of food for the flower inside it.

If you cut a bulb in half you can see the tiny plant already formed inside. As the plant grows it uses up the layers of food inside the bulb.

Some other plants that grow from bulbs are lilies, daffodils and gladiolas. If you plant bulbs outdoors in the Fall, you will have colorful flowers in the Spring.

*An onion is one kind of bulb.

Tulips
Tulips come in many colors!

Plant tulip bulbs in rich,* well-drained soil. Spade the ground. Dig holes 4-6 inches deep, 6 inches apart. Put the bulbs in the holes (one in each hole) and cover them with soil.

Gophers like to eat bulbs. To protect your bulb you can cover it with $\frac{1}{4}$ inch wire mesh before you plant it.

*Get adult help with digging, and with adding nutrients to the soil.

Flower log:

Plant bulbs in the Fall.

Flowers will bloom in early Spring.

There are many kinds of tulips!

118

Daffodils
Come in mixtures of yellow, white, orange.

Plant bulbs in early Fall. Plant large bulbs 5-6 inches deep, small ones 4-5 inches deep. Plant them 8 inches apart. Cover with soil. Water well after planting.

If you have gophers in your garden, protect your bulbs with wire mesh.

Flower log:
Plant in full sun.
Water plants well (unless rains come).
Flowers bloom in early Spring

119

Marigolds

Marigolds can be yellow, gold, orange, brown, maroon.

Marigolds are easy to grow from seed, or you can buy small plants already started.

Plant seeds 10-15 inches apart, $\frac{1}{4}$ inch deep. Keep well watered. Flowers grow to 12-18 inches high, or 36-48 inches high depending on what kind of Marigolds you plant.

Marigolds are good flowers to cut and put in the house in a vase or container you like.

Flower log:
Plant in full sun.

Marigolds are a good border plant.

Pansies

White, yellow, pink, purple, violet color mixtures.

Plant the pansy seeds in early Spring or in the Fall. Plant them $\frac{1}{16}$ inch deep. Thin the plants to 3 inches apart when they are 1 inch tall.

Pansies add lots of color to your yard. You can pick them too, and enjoy the flowers indoors.

Flower log:
Plant in rich, moist soil.
Plant in full sun near the coast, in some shade in warmer climates.

Keep the pansies well watered by soaking the ground around the plants.

121

Petunias
Come in lavendar, pink, red, purple, white, blue.

Flower log:
Plant in full sun.
Petunias have long-lasting flowers
Hardy plants- good for borders.

Plant petunia seeds 8-18 inches apart. Keep well watered. Water your plants near the soil, not on the flowers.

Petunias can grow to about 24 inches high, depending on what kind you plant. There are very small kinds too.

I'm a little petunia in an onion patch....

Growing Flowers

Here are some other flowers you can grow from seeds. There are many more....

Zinnias

Mexican Sunflower

Poppy

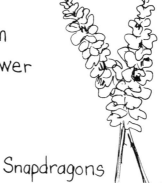

Snapdragons

Morning Glories

Nasturtium

Grow'em and Eat 'em

One of the fun things about planting fruits and vegetables is that you can enjoy growing things and eating them too!

Before planting fruits and vegetables, prepare your soil following directions in Chapter 10. Some plants may need fertilizer. Get adult help for this.

Happy planting!

Radishes

Radishes grow very fast!

Plant radish seeds in smooth, raked soil. Plant seeds $\frac{1}{2}$ inch deep, in rows 1 or 2 feet apart. Firm the soil down over the planted seeds. When the plants start growing, thin them to 1 inch apart. Keep the ground moist. If you want fresh radishes all the time, sow a few seeds every week.

Wash the radishes, and eat them fresh and crunchy.

radish seeds

Lettuce
Loose - leaf type

Plant lettuce seeds in well-drained soil and in full sun. Rake the soil so it does not have any lumps. Scatter the seeds in rows. Cover and firm the soil over the seeds. In about 6-10 days you should begin to see sprouts.

Thin the small plants to 8-12 inches apart. You should be able to pick leaves for your salad in 7-9 weeks.

Pick the outside leaves as the lettuce grows. (The plant will keep growing more)! This will give you lettuce for many weeks.

Plant log:
Plant in early Spring
Plant seeds $\frac{1}{4}$ inch deep, 15-18 inches between rows

Wash it, <u>then</u> eat!

127

Carrots

Plant carrot seeds in loose, fluffy soil. Plant seeds ½ inch deep, 2 inches apart.

Carrots take a long time to

Plant log:

Plant in early Spring.

Takes 65-75 days for full-grown carrots

Keep soil moist. Spray lightly when watering.

Carrots (cont.)

push through the ground into the light. Don't give up!

Thin the carrot plants when the tops are 2-3 inches tall. Thin them again 1 month later, (leaving bigger spaces between remaining plants).

This time you will be able to eat these small tender carrots! Delicious!

The remaining carrots can be picked when 6-7 inches long. (Test one and see).

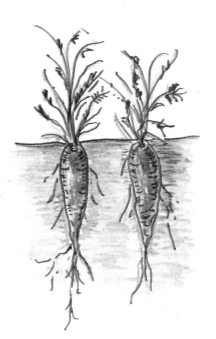

Tomatoes

You can grow tomatoes from seeds, or buy seedlings (little tomato plants). There are many kinds of tomatoes - large or small. Pick the kind that is best for you.

stake →

If you live in a cold climate it is a good idea to buy seedlings or to plant your seeds in the house first. You can transplant these outside when the weather is warm.

Plant log:
Plant outside only when weather and ground are warm - no frost!
Little cherry tomatoes are fun to grow and eat.
Harvest in 11-16 weeks.

Tomatoes (cont.)

To plant tomato seeds outside find a sunny spot with good drainage. Plant the seeds ¼ inch deep, 3-4 feet apart. Water well.

The tomato plant is a vine plant. The vines should be kept off the ground. To do this, put a 6 foot stake by each plant. Tie the plant loosely to the stake as it grows.

Keep your tomato plant well watered. Water the ground only so the leaves don't get wet. Pick tomatoes when they are red and firm.

Green Onions
Great in salad!

Plant onion seeds in loose, well-drained soil. Keep weeds out! Have the soil smooth and raked well. Plant the seeds $\frac{1}{2}$ inch deep in rows about 18 inches apart. Press soil firmly over the seeds.

Plant log:
Plant seeds in early Spring.

Pull up onions in 13-16 weeks

Thin plants when they are about 3 inches high. Keep the soil raked around the onion plants. Keep soil moist. Never let it dry out.

You can buy onion bulbs (sets) instead of seeds. Plant all Winter through April in mild climate. Plant in Spring in harsh climates.

132

Seeds on a Sponge

Cress sandwiches are good - Cress grows fast this way!

You need:
Sponge (or wet towel or tissue)
Package of cress seeds
Saucer or plastic toy

Soak the sponge in water and put it on a saucer. (Any container will work - It's fun to put the sponge in a plastic toy you like such as a basket, egg or truck). Sprinkle cress seeds on top of the damp sponge. This works with other kinds of seeds too! Press the seeds down gently so they will be dampened. Keep the sponge moist. Check it every day.

When the leaves start to grow put the container in a sunny window. Harvest when the plants are about 1 inch high. Cut off the leaves with a scissors. Cress is good in salad or on bread with butter.

Cucumbers

Plant cucumber seeds in your garden in a warm, sunny spot. Plant seeds in rows or little hills with 6-8 seeds 🌱. Firm the soil over your seeds. There should be 3-4 feet between hills.

You should see little seedlings 6-8 days after planting. Thin your cucumber plants. Leave the 3 best ones. They need lots of room to spread out! The cucumbers should be ready to eat in about 6 weeks.

Plant log:
Plant in late Spring when soil is very warm.

Plant seeds
$\frac{1}{2}$ inch deep.

Vine plant - needs room.

Peanut Plant
Grows best in warm places

Soak the peanuts in water overnight. Take the shells off carefully. Do not tear the brown covering over the nut.

Plant large Virginia peanuts 10 inches apart, 2 inches deep. Plant Spanish peanuts 5 inches apart, 2 inches deep. Water well. In about 2 weeks you should see the top growth of the plants. Flowers

Plant log:
This plant needs lots of sunlight.
Plant in early Spring from shelled unroasted peanuts. (Get them from a health food store)
Soil should be fluffy and light-textured.
Harvest in 110-120 days.

Peanut Plant (cont.)

will appear on the plants. When the flowers drop off, pegs develop. The pegs drop into the soil to ripen.

Keep your plants well-watered until 2 weeks before harvest. In about $3\frac{1}{2}$ months your peanut plants will be ready to pick.

Loosen the soil around each plant. Pull up the plant and shake the dirt off the peanuts. The peanuts will be on the vine. Put them in a warm, dry place out of the sunlight for 2-3 weeks. Then pick the peanuts off the vine.

peg

peanut seeds

roots →

Roasting Peanuts

To roast the peanuts in the shell turn the oven to 300°. Put peanuts in a shallow baking pan with a thin layer of cooking oil. Roast for 1 hour, stirring occasionally.

Take 'em out, cool a bit, then eat 'em! Yum!

Popcorn
Plant at least 3 rows for pollination.

Plant popcorn seeds in a sunny spot. Plant them 12 inches apart. Leave 18-24 inches between rows. Water well. Do not plant regular corn near the popcorn or the corn will be tough.

Pick the corn when the stalks are brown and dried out. Leave the husks on. Store the popcorn ears in a cool, dry place for about 1 month. Then take off the hard kernels. Store them in a covered jar until popping time.

Plant log:
Order popcorn seeds from a seed company (Address on p.176).
Plant seeds in early Spring
Popcorn takes a long time to grow—at least 3 months.

Pumpkins
Make Jack O' Lanterns for Halloween!

Plant pumpkin seeds in a large, warm, sunny area. Make sure the soil is lump free and sandy. For giant pumpkins, plant Big Max seeds or other giant type.

Plant 6-8 seeds 1 inch deep in hills. This will make 1 set of pumpkin vines. For more

Plant log:

Pumpkins take a lot of room to grow!

Plant seeds in May or June.

Pick pumpkins in Fall in time for Halloween.

Pumpkins (cont.)

pumpkins plant more hills, 8 feet apart. Water the seeds after planting. Thin when plants get 2-3 inches in size.

Be careful not to water the pumpkin vines. Water around the little hills. Leave only 3-4 pumpkins on the vines. If you want a super big one, leave only one! Leave the pumpkins nearest the plant when you pick. Pick off the ones you don't want from the last part of the vine.

Happy Halloweening!

Roast Pumpkin Seeds

Wash your pumpkin seeds in cold water. Drain and dry them on paper towels. Put them in a shallow baking pan. Set your oven at 250° and slowly brown them. Watch them carefully. Take them out when they are light brown.

Pumpkin seeds have lots of oil. If you feel they need more, drizzle a little oil on them. Salt and eat!

Sunflowers
Seeds are good to eat!

Plant your sunflower seeds in full sun when the ground is warm. Soil should be moist.

This plant grows 6-12 feet tall! The flower gets very big too! Plant it behind other plants because it gets so tall.

After the flower blooms gather the seeds. Dry the sunflower seeds under the broiler. (See Mom for this!) Salt and cool the seeds. They are fun to eat!

Plant log:
Fast growing
Plant seeds $\frac{1}{2}$ inch deep, 12 inches apart.
Blooms in late Summer.

Gourds
Funny to look at - but don't eat!

Plant gourd seeds ½ inch deep when the ground is warm. Press down well. When plants are a few inches tall, thin out. Leave about 12 inches between plants. Let the vines climb on wire, fences, or on a trellis. ⚘

After picking gourds, store in a cool, dry place so they can dry out. Coat them with shellac if you want to keep them a long time. Gourds make good plant containers!

Plant log:
Climbing vines with beautiful leaves and odd shaped fruits.
Good for decorations and toys.
Harvest gourds when they feel firm.

145

Bean Sprouts
You can grow this crop indoors!

Get Mung beans at a grocery store, Oriental shop, or order from a seed company. They grow very fast. You can eat them in 5 days!

Wash $\frac{1}{2}$ cup of beans. Soak them overnight in cold water. Drain beans. Put them in a screwtop jar with holes punched in the lid. Cover the jar with a cloth to keep out the light. Put it in a dark place. Rinse the beans with water and drain them. Do this 2 or 3 times a day.

Bean sprouts are good in salads or stir-fried with other vegetables in salad oil. (Get help with the cooking part).

Swiss Chard

Plant Swiss Chard seeds $\frac{1}{2}$ inch deep in a sunny spot. Leave 18-24 inches between rows. When seedlings appear thin plants to 12 inches apart.

Water the plants well. Pick the outside leaves as they grow. The plant will grow more. You can begin to harvest in about 60 days.

Plant log:
Can be grown any time of year in mild climate. Plant seeds in early Spring in places with cold Winters.

Crookneck Squash

Plant log:
Plant seeds
1 inch deep.

Plants grow
in 7-8 weeks.

Squash needs
room to grow.

Plant squash seeds in Spring, when the ground is warm. Plant them in little hills, 6-8 seeds to a hill. Firm the soil over the seeds. Spray well with water. In about 6-10 days your small plants should start to grow.

Thin out the plants, leaving about 3 of the best. Water the plants around the bottom of the hill. Squash

Crookneck Squash (cont.)

is a vine plant. Try not

to get the plant too wet. Pick squash when 3-4 inches long.

Cantaloupe
Also called Muskmelon

Plant cantaloupe seeds in late Spring when the ground is warm. The soil should be raked and fertilized.* Cantaloupes take $2\frac{1}{2}$-4 months of heat to ripen.

Plant seeds in hills, 6-8 seeds to a hill. Firm the soil over the seeds. Water with a light spray. Thin the plants when they come up. Leave the best 3 on each hill. When you water, water around the hills so the vine will not get too wet. Your cantaloupe will taste much better than those in the store!

Plant log:
Cantaloupes need lots of heat and lots of room.
Plant in little hills 4-6 feet apart.
Pick in 75-90 days.

* Get adult help.

Strawberries

Plan a strawberry patch or get a "strawberry pot". It has pockets to hold the plants.

Buy June-bearing strawberry plants. Plant them in early Spring. You will get small berries the first year. Protect the plants with a plastic covering all Winter. Next year you will have a bigger crop!

To plant, put gravel on the bottom of the pot. Add soil. When you come to a pocket, tuck in a plant. Water as you go. Make sure the "crown" (the part dividing top and roots) is at ground level. Enjoy your berries!

151

Seed Science

Watch a Seed Come to Life!

If you use a lima bean soak it until you can take the outside cover off.

It is fun to look at the insides with a magnifying glass. You can see the root and tiny leaves of the plant.

food for the plant → ← tiny leaves
root ↗

Wet a piece of blotter paper and put it in a glass. Put the beans or seeds against the glass, in front of the paper. Keep the paper moist by adding just a tiny bit of water at the bottom of the glass. Don't let the paper dry out.

You need:
Drinking glass or clear plastic cup
Lima beans or squash or radish seeds
Magnifying glass
Blotter paper or construction paper

Watch a Seed Come to Life! (cont.)

The roots of the new plant will grow down to find food for the plant. The stem will push up. It will get leaves and push out into the sunlight. The halves of the beans will wither as the food is used up.

When your new plant gets roots, pot it in soil.

stem → leaves

roots →

← leaves

Crystal Garden
These crystals "grow" like plants

You need adult help for handling chemicals. Put briquettes in the pan. Mix the water, salt, bluing and ammonia in a bowl. Pour it over the briquettes. Make sure some pieces of the briquettes stick out of the solution. Within 1 hour crystals form. Soon they will cover the briquettes. (Don't handle them — they are fragile).

You need:
- 2-3 charcoal briquettes
- Throw-away pan and bowl
- $\frac{1}{4}$ cup salt
- $\frac{1}{4}$ cup laundry bluing
- 1 tablespoon ammonia
- Adult help!

crystals forming

briquettes

bluing, salt and ammonia mixture

155

Plant - Light Experiment

You need:
shoebox
milk carton
sprouted plant -
bean or
potato

Cut a small hole in one side of the shoe-box. Stand it upright. Put the plant inside, on top of the milk carton. Put the cover on the shoebox. Put it where the hole will get a lot of light.

Take a peek every day. You will see the plant growing toward the light. Turn the plant. It will grow toward the light every time!

Red Celery and Green Carnations
(Use other colors of food coloring if you like).

Plants need water to live and grow. Water moves up to the leaves of plants through tiny tubes from the roots and stems. You can almost see the water move up the plant when you do these experiments.

Get a fresh stalk of celery with leaves on top. Cut an inch off the bottom and put the stalk in a glass of water. Add red food coloring until the water turns red. In about half an hour you will see the celery leaves change color.

celery, red food coloring, and water

green carnation

You can make green carnations this way too with water and green food coloring.

157

Making Cactus Cuttings

One way to have a big cactus collection is to make more plants from those you have. To do this, cut a piece off your cactus.* Let the cut end dry out away from the sunlight for 3-4 days. Then put the piece of cactus (cut end down) in a pot to root. Plant it $\frac{1}{2}$ inch deep in the layer of sand. Water just a bit.

You need:
Cactus plants
Pot full of cactus potting soil —
Make top inch a layer of sand - (Not ocean sand!)

*When cutting the piece off your cactus, cut the top off if the plant is a tall column. ᶜᵘᵗ
If the plant has pods, or branches, cut off a whole segment. ᶜᵘᵗ

Cactus Grafting
Get help with cutting if you need it.

Cactus plants can attach themselves and grow on other cacti. This is called grafting. You can make some strange combinations this way! You can even graft lots of different cacti onto 1 cactus plant. When you graft you create plants not found in nature.

The easiest way to graft cactus is to use tall columnar plants. Cut the tops off both plants. Switch tops. Hold the pieces of your new plants together with rubber bands or string. Leave it on about 2 weeks (until your graft "takes").

Plant Art
(Designs from Nature)

This chapter has ideas for things to make and do using objects from nature. Keep a collection of natural things – you can find many uses for them. Here are some things that are good to save for projects:

seeds   pine cones   shells
seed pods   driftwood   nuts
feathers   flowers and   acorns
dried weeds   leaves

Be sure to have permission before gathering things on private property, and protect plants and animals you see. (Be good to Mother Nature....)

Gourd Maracas

Maracas are a musical instrument. To make them from gourds poke a nail hole in the stem and end of the gourd. This helps the gourd to dry out faster.

When the gourd is dry the seeds are loose. They make a noise when you shake the "maracas". Spray or paint with shellac (get adult help) to preserve your gourds.

162

Drying Flowers

You need:
2 cups Borax
2 cups yellow cornmeal
3 tablespoons salt
---
wire shoebox

Some flowers dry by themselves, but most need a drying agent to preserve them. Mix the recipe. Put 1-inch of the powder in a box lined with wax paper.

Pick the flowers for drying on a sunny day. Pick flowers not fully developed. Cut off the stems 1 inch below the flower. Replace stems with wire. Run the wire up through the flower. Dry flat flowers face down. Dry other flowers

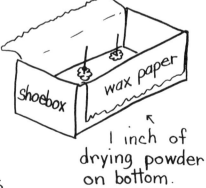

shoebox

wax paper

1 inch of drying powder on bottom.

Drying Flowers (cont.)

petals up (bend the wire). Sprinkle the drying agent lightly over the flowers. Just barely cover the flowers. Cover the box and put it where it won't be disturbed. Drying takes 10 days – 3 weeks.

Brush off the drying powder gently. Put the flowers in your favorite container. If you like, wrap green florists tape around the wire stems. (Or dry foliage separately and put stems and flowers back together when dry)

Fruit and Vegetable Printing

Some vegetables and fruits make exciting artwork to hang on your wall!

All you do is cut them in half, paint them with ink or paint and press them on paper.

lemon

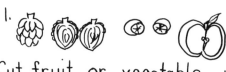

1. Cut fruit or vegetable in half.

2. Paint or ink it.

3. Press on paper (paint side down) to print.

166

Fruit and Vegetable Printing (cont.)

Artichokes make beautiful prints. Apples, mushrooms, oranges, lemons are good too. If you want interesting designs, cut patterns into potatoes or carrots, then print.

artichoke

potato

mushroom

Leaf Rubbings

Rubbings are fun and easy to make. Peel the papers off your crayons. Put the leaves under the paper, hold everything still and rub with your crayon. The imprint of the leaf will come through.

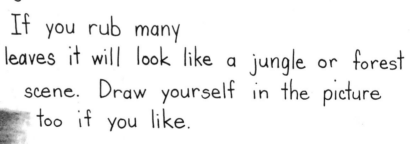

If you rub many leaves it will look like a jungle or forest scene. Draw yourself in the picture too if you like.

Jungle Rubbing

Pressed Leaves and Flowers
There are many ways to use these!

Pick leaves and flowers without dew on them. Fold newspapers and put the plants between the folds. Arrange them the way you want them. They will dry the way you leave them. Put heavy books on top of the folded newspaper. In about a week your flowers will be dry and ready to decorate with.

You can use these flowers many ways — glue them in notebooks, put them on stationary, arrange them in frames, decorate Valentines, etc. Another good project is to put them between 2 pieces of clear, stick-on plastic. You can invent other uses too!

Peanut Puppet Heads

You need:
Peanut shells
Cut paper or
 fabric scraps
Glue
Marking pens
Scissors

Carefully break the ends off peanut shells. Shake the nuts out. Decorate the peanut shells any way you like. They make great finger puppets!

You can cut a hole in a box for a puppet theater.

SHOW TODAY

Plant Pests

Pests can be a real problem to plants. Check both indoor and garden plants often for pests. Check plants very carefully before buying them too. A healthy plant will have less chance of being "buggy."

Here are some pests that might be on your plants, indoors or out. There are many ways to deal with them. The best thing to do is get adult help right away.

snails

cutworms

white flies

red spider mites

Plant Pests (cont.)

 scales

 aphids

 thrips

 mealy bugs

If there are lots of pests on your plant, it is best to throw it away. Wash your hands, tools, and flower pot and start again. Then at least your other plants won't get "buggy."

Try not to be too upset loosing a plant because of pests. This can happen to anyone who has plants.

Sick Plants

Here are some things you can try if your plant looks sick and droopy. Sometimes they help.

Turn a glass jar upside down over your plant, or cover it with a big plastic bag. The cover keeps the air moist. This may be what the plant needs to come back to good health.

If you have a crack in a clay flower pot, here is something to do to fix it. Light a candle (get adult help)! Then pour candle wax in the crack. Presto! Your pot is fixed!

Help for You

Here are some places you can write for seed, plant, and garden catalogs:

Armstrong Associates, Inc.
Box 127
Basking Ridge, New Jersey 07920

Venus Fly-traps

W. Atlee Burpee Co.
Philadelphia, Pa. 19132
or   Clinton, Iowa   52732
or   Riverside, Calif. 92502

Vegetables, berries,
midget fruits and
vegetables, Venus
Fly-traps, popcorn

Help for You (cont.)

John Brundy's Rare Plant House
Box 34
Cocoa Beach, Florida 32931

Cobra Lily
Catalog is 50¢.

Burgess Seed and Plant Co.
Galesburg, Michigan

Midget and other fruits
and vegetables. Several
kinds of mini-tomatoes

George W. Park, Seed Co, Inc.
Greenwood, So. Carolina 29646

Vegetables, herbs,
midget fruits and
vegetables

Help for You (cont.)

Wildflower Gardening   Wildflower seeds
P.O. Box 2091
Castro Valley, Calif. 94546

Other places to go for help are:

1. Your County Agricultural Agent.
2. A nearby college with classes about plants.
3. Botannical Garden, if there is one in your area.
4. Horticultural or plant societies.
5. A nearby nursery or expert in your neighborhood.

Index

Adventures in Gardening

Grow 'em Outdoors

Growing Flowers

Grow 'em and Eat 'em

Nitty Gritty Productions appreciates the artistic efforts of the following young artists whose drawings appear in this book:

Patricia Ala p. 25
Sherri Arriola p. 17
Michelle Bissell pp. 40 and
  Next to Title Page
Colleen Buckley pp. 61, 133,
  160 and Last Page in Book
Marc Buckley and
  Kenny McDonell p. 68
Ed Calibjo p. 5
Maria Campos p. 152
Linda Disalvo p. 100

Dale Duncan p. 144
Mirian Fernandez p. 76
Nancy Gill pp. 52, 116
Brian Morgan pp. 92, 124
Leonardo Oceguera p. 32
Kathy Papadopoulos p. 88
Sariel Reynoso pp. 12, 108, and
  First Page in Book
Anna Rivas pp. 45 and
  Next to Introduction
Cheryl Shelmadine pp. 165, 172